# House Buying 101

## *14 Things You Should Know BEFORE You Buy Your Home*

by

Pamela D. Pitts
Butterfly Financial, LLC

Copyright © 2009 Butterfly Financial, LLC
www.ButterflyFinancialLLC.com

Pamela D. Pitts, Author
Layout, Design & Cover Design by:
Lucy Richardson, New Visions Technical Solutions

All rights reserved, including the right of reproduction in whole or in part in any form.

ISBN 978-0-578-03994-7

## *Disclaimer*

This book is intended for educational purposes only. Information in this book should be used as a guide only and should not be relied upon as the sole source of information relating to its content. No warranty, either express or implied, is made with respect to the information contained herein. Neither Pamela D. Pitts nor Butterfly Financial, LLC, is responsible for any loss, inconvenience, damage (whether special or consequential) or claims arising out of the use of the information contained in this book.

## *Contents*

*pg*

#1   House Buying: How Much Can You Afford?.................................... 7

#2   How Important Is Your Credit Score? ………......…..………. 9

#3   Should You Pre-qualify for A Loan? …….....………......………. 11

#4   Why Should You Obtain A Reputable Real Estate Agent? ….......... 13

#5   How Do You Go About Finding A Home Loan? ......….....……….. 15

#6   Why Shop for Lowest Interest Rate On A Home Mortgage? ......... 17

#7   Should You Obtain A 15 Year Or 30 Year Mortgage? …............….. 19

#8   Should You Make A Down Payment? ……..….....………………. 21

#9   Should You Obtain A Home Inspection And Home Warranty? …... 23

#10  What Is The Importance Of An Appraisal? ………….…...…… 25

#11  Should Property Taxes Be Paid Separately? ………………… 27

#12  Should You Set Aside Money For Decorating, Furnishing And Home Improvements? ………..…..………………………….... 29

#13  What Are Appreciation And Depreciation? ……….…..………... 31

#14  What Are Closing Costs? ………………......………………. 33

Glossary ……………………………………….…………….. 35

Sources/Resources ……………………………….…………. 37

# *Forward*

You're thinking about buying a house but you're not sure what is involved. This book can help. Many of us remember our first home purchase as being a time of uncertainty. We weren't sure where to start and what the process entailed. We may have relied on the well-meaning advice of friends and family, only to realize later that some of the advice could have been a bit better. You don't have to have the same experience.

In this book, some of the main questions which need to be considered, both before and during a home purchase, are asked and answered. The information is straight forward and intended to help you skillfully navigate your way through the home buying process.

# #1
## House Buying: How Much Can You Afford?

YOU THINK YOU'RE READY to buy a house? What do you need to do before you move forward? Find your dream house? Not quite. You should determine how much you can afford to spend on housing costs. Why should this be the first step? This will prevent you from getting in over your head or attempting to buy a house you can't afford.

How do you determine how much you can afford to pay for a house? The Department of Housing and Urban Development provides that the generally accepted definition of affordability is for a household to pay no more than 30% of its annual income in housing. Oh, by the way, that's 30% of after tax income. Meaning that you should not spend more than 30% of your after tax income to pay for house related costs. Now I know what you're thinking, 30% isn't very much. Remember, this is a conservative estimate designed to ensure you have money available for other needs and wants.

Why is it so important to limit your

*Borrowers often begin their home search with only the foggiest idea about how much they can afford to pay, which can result in wasted time and frustration. They should know approximately how much they can afford before they start to shop.*

housing costs to 30% of your after tax income? So that you will have money left over for other basic needs such as food, transportation, and healthcare, not to mention a little fun. Limiting the amount of money you spend on house related needs will also ensure that you have the ability to save money for education and invest for retirement.

What type of housing related costs should you be expected to cover with 30% of your after tax income? You should be able to pay for the mortgage principal, the interest on the mortgage, home insurance, property taxes, household maintenance and utilities (electricity, gas and water).

---

There is **no magic dollar amount** that you should be looking for regarding the "perfect home". How much house you can afford is as unique as you are; it's based on many factors, including your location, income, savings, personal preferences, and most importantly, the house-buying plan you have in place.

Here's a **quick checklist of important questions** to review as you consider how much house you can afford. If you cannot answer YES to these questions regarding the house you have your eye on, then it may not be a wise move to buy it right now.

- Can I make at least a 10% (preferably a 20%) down payment?
- Can I keep house payments at or below 25% of my monthly take-home pay?
- Am I working closely with a real estate agent I can trust?

*Source: www.daveramsey.com*

# #2
## How Important Is Your Credit Score?

WHAT IS CREDIT? The use of credit occurs when you are loaned money. In other words, when you buy something on credit, you are borrowing money. Examples of using credit include getting a loan for a car, house, or simply buying something using a credit card. The bottom line is you're using someone else's money to get something you want.

Not everyone is allowed to have credit. Why not? They don't have a good credit score. What is a credit score? Your credit score is the number creditors use to help determine whether to give you credit, and the interest rate you will be charged for the credit. If a person does not have a good credit score, loaning them money is seen as being risky. Would you want to loan money to someone if they had a history of not repaying the money or they always paid you later than they said they would? Probably not. Well, neither do credit card companies or other lenders.

Why is a good credit score important when purchasing a home? Your credit score tells others how well you have handled the credit

> *A higher credit score will result in a better (lower) interest rate. Make sure you are paying your bills on time and not taking on too much debt. Also, get a copy of your credit report and review it a few times a year to ensure it is accurate. If you find errors, promptly take the necessary steps to correct them.*

that has been given to you in the past. For example, did you make your payments on time every month? If you did, this will positively affect your credit score! If you didn't, this will have a negative impact on your score. A higher credit score means that you should be able to obtain a lower interest rate on your home loan. A lower interest rate means greater savings for you over the years while you are making payments on your home loan.

Your credit score is a number ranging between 300 and 850. The best score you can have is 850. You want to keep your score as high as possible. Why? It will be easier for you to obtain credit in the future and also, if you need to, you will be able to borrow money at a lower interest rate for home and car loans. Some insurance companies check out your credit score and use it to determine the amount you will pay for car and home insurance. Lenders use it to decide if you are either creditworthy or a credit risk. Some employers and landlords use your credit score to make hiring and renting decisions.

Information from your credit report is used to determine your credit score. Your credit score will contain information on your loan and payment history regarding your car loans, student loans, credit cards, home loans and so on. It's your job to make sure you handle loans and credit cards wisely and responsibly. Be sure to obtain a copy of your credit report and correct any errors before applying for a home loan.

*Credit Score Factors >>*

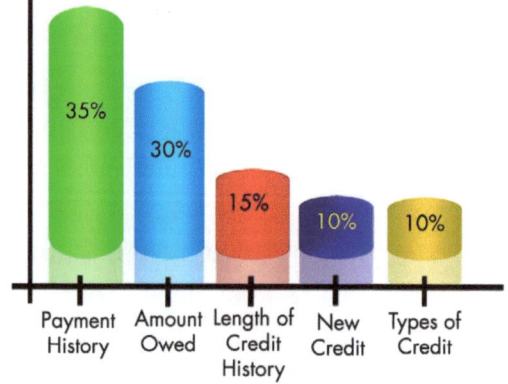

# #3
## Should You Pre-qualify For A Loan?

WHAT DOES PRE-QUALIFICATION involve? Pre-qualification means that you get a rough estimate from a lender regarding how much the lender will allow you to borrow. Many lenders will allow you to do this over the phone and will generally not charge a fee. Be aware that pre-qualification does not mean the lender will definitely provide you with a loan. Pre-qualification simply gives you a ball park estimate regarding the amount of loan you may potentially be able to obtain. Some real estate agents will not work with you if you have not been pre-qualified for a loan.

*A loan pre-qualification can aid a homebuyer in the purchase of a home because it gives the buyer a clearer picture of how much money can be spent toward the purchase of the home. As a buyer with loan pre-qualification, the homebuyer has the option of negotiating a better price or a reasonable payment plan with the seller.*

When you are ready to get serious about house hunting, you may want to consider getting pre-approved for a loan. During the pre-approval process, the lender will check your credit history and obtain an understanding of your outstanding debt. You will also be required to verify your income and in some cases, your work history. As part of the pre-approval process you will have to submit an application and pay a fee. Once this information has been reviewed, the lender will

let you know how much money you may borrow for the purchase of a home.

Before you go through the pre-approval process, you should obtain and review your credit report. Look to make sure all information contained in your credit report is accurate. If you find any inaccurate information, promptly contact the credit bureaus: Experian, Equifax, and Transunion to ensure that any discrepancies are corrected. The bureaus are supposed to make any necessary corrections within a 30 day period. Remember, your credit score will affect the interest rate you are able to obtain for your home loan. The higher your credit score, the lower the interest rate; which means the overall cost of your loan will be lower.

---

**Is Loan Pre-qualification Good Enough?**

Loan pre-qualification in all circumstances is a good thing to have. Being pre-qualified means a lender has deemed the borrower an adequate credit risk and has qualified the borrower for a loan. Although the specific terms of the loan the borrower needs relative to the purchase have not been set, the borrower has a range in which to work and negotiate with the seller.

---

*Source: www.loan.com*

# #4
# Why Should You Obtain A Reputable Real Estate Agent?

YOU'RE READY TO PURCHASE a home and you're thinking about looking for the home on your own. Think again. Consider using the services of a knowledgeable real estate agent. Why? The agent will be helpful in identifying prospective houses for purchase. The agent will also assist you in preparing and presenting an offer once you find a home you're interested in. Also, the agent will work on your behalf to negotiate the deal.

Agents can be helpful in many ways. For instance, agents generally have established relationships with other professionals whose services may be required in a real estate transaction such as lawyers, home inspectors, and mortgage brokers.

You want to ensure that you use a trustworthy, reputable agent. Ask the agent for the contact information of three recent clients. Contact the clients and ask about their experience with the agent. You may want to ask how long the agent has worked as a real estate

> *Meet agents out in their working environment, not in their offices. Good agents spend very little time at their desks.*
>
> *A good place to meet agents is at open houses. Don't worry that you are not interested in that particular property. Another good method is to contact the agent with whom a friend or relative worked. If this agent produced positive results for a friend of yours, there's a good chance s/he will do the same for you.*

agent. However, the length of time an agent has worked in real estate does not necessarily determine his/her ability. Be sure you reach an agreement with the agent at the outset regarding how the agent will keep you informed about the progress of your transaction.

Generally, you will not be responsible for compensating the agent; this is the responsibility of the seller. The agent will either be compensated based on a flat fee or a commission. If the compensation is by way of commission, the commission will be based on a percentage of the sales price.

**Good real estate agents are worth their weight in gold!**

Good real estate agents must get along well with buyers and sellers. It helps if real estate agents are pleasant and dress neatly. They should be well organized and be able to remember people's names. They should deal honestly with people and have good manners.

*Source: www.infoplease.com*

# #5
## How Do You Go About Finding A Home Loan?

NOW THAT YOU HAVE FOUND a house you like and determined that you can afford it, what's next? You will need to find a way to finance the purchase of the home by obtaining a home loan. There are several different sources for home loans including banks, credit unions, and mortgage brokers. You can shop for home loans on the internet or by directly speaking with several lenders. Many different types of home loans are available. The loans will usually vary based on length of time and interest rate.

There are loans available with fixed interest rates. Fixed interest rates are typically better because your monthly payment will remain fixed throughout the life of the loan. You'll always know what you're going to pay. However, your mortgage payment will change somewhat if your property taxes or home insurance premium change.

There are also loans with variable interest rates known typically as adjustable rate

> *Before you put your signature on any loan papers, be sure the company you are dealing with has a good reputation in the home mortgage loan community. You can check with the Better Business Bureau as well as do a bit of research on the company from which you are thinking of borrowing money. Once again the internet can help you. You can find reviews from previous customers to find out how they liked working with a certain lender.*

mortgages. These loans will involve changes to your monthly mortgage payment whenever the interest rate on the mortgage adjusts or changes. A change in the mortgage payment could have a negative impact on your ability to pay the mortgage and could jeopardize your ownership of the home. For this reason, please be sure you understand the specific requirements of an adjustable rate mortgage before signing the contract for the mortgage.

Once you approach the lenders, they will determine how much they are willing to lend you. How do lenders determine how much they are willing to lend you? One of the factors lenders consider is your debt-to-income ratio. What's that? It's a comparison of your monthly debt payments and monthly household income. What are debt payments? It's money you pay every month on your credit cards, student loans, car loans etc. The general debt-to-income ratio lenders are looking for is 36%. This means all of the money you pay out every month on total debt, including your mortgage payment should not exceed 36% of your after tax income. If you want to increase your ability to obtain a higher loan amount, it would be wise for you to reduce the balance owed on some of your other monthly debt.

> ***Warning:*** When the easy money was flowing, you could get a great deal on a mortgage from just about anyone. But in today's credit-challenged world, all the avenues for finding a mortgage come with their own set of obstacles.
>
> Many banks have tightened lending standards and scaled back offerings. Some banks are no longer working with mortgage brokers, who are under fire for pushing bad loans during the boom.
>
> And while online lending sites hold the promise of one-stop shopping, some have developed a reputation for playing bait-and-switch on rates and not fully disclosing fees.
>
> **Scour the Web, Go directly to a bank, Call on a broker**

*Source: money.cnn.com*

# #6

# Why Shop For Lowest Interest Rate On A Home Mortgage?

WHY IS IT SO IMPORTANT for you to obtain the lowest interest rate possible on a home loan? More of your monthly mortgage payment will go toward paying off your house and less will be received by the lender as interest. When you obtain a home loan, you will have to pay interest on the loan. The interest represents the return on the investment the lender will receive as a result of making the loan to you.

Let's take a look at an example. Suppose you want to borrow $200,000 to purchase a house that costs $220,000. You decide to shop for a loan because you either don't have cash or do not want to pay for the house with cash. The first lender you approach is willing to loan you $200,000 but will charge 7% interest for a 30 year loan. The second lender will also loan you the money but will charge 6% interest for a 30 year loan. Which is a better deal and why? The 6% loan is better and here's the reason: Your monthly payment with the 6% loan will be $1,193.13. Your monthly payment with the 7% loan will be $1,322.80. That means with the 6%

> *Shopping around for a home loan or mortgage will help you to get the best financing deal. A mortgage--whether it's a home purchase, a refinancing, or a home equity loan--is a product, just like a car, so the price and terms may be negotiable. You'll want to compare all the costs involved in obtaining a mortgage. Shopping, comparing, and negotiating may save you thousands of dollars.*

loan you save $129.67 ($1,322.80-$1,193.13) every month. That's money you can invest in a retirement account or put toward the payment of credit card debt. How much money will you be able to save over the 30 year period of the loan? You will save over $46,000!

Be sure to shop for a home loan. Doing so will help you find a competitive interest rate for your loan. Also, be aware that your credit score will affect the interest rate you are able to obtain from a lender.

#7

## Should You Obtain A 15 Year Or 30 Year Mortgage?

YOU'RE READY TO BUY a house but really can't decide whether you should finance the mortgage over 15 years or 30 years. How do you decide? What are the advantages and disadvantages? First, the interest rate you can obtain for a 15 year loan will be less than the interest rate you can obtain for a 30 year loan. Why do lenders charge a lower interest rate for a 15 year loan? Primarily because the lender is loaning money for a shorter period of time which means the lender will get its money back quicker and be able to invest it elsewhere. However, with a 30 year loan, the lender's money is unavailable for twice as many years and the lender is missing out on the opportunity to invest the money elsewhere. To compensate for the lost opportunity, the lender charges a higher interest rate for the 30 year loan.

Here's another factor to consider. Although your interest rate will be lower with a 15 year loan, your monthly payments will be higher. Why? You're paying off your loan much quicker with a 15 year loan so naturally the monthly payments will be higher. The good

> *The truth is that there is no one "answer" to the 30-year versus 15-year mortgage debate. What works best for one homeowner may not work best for another.*

news is that your equity will increase faster as well. What is equity? Equity is the current market value of a home minus the outstanding mortgage balance. Essentially, it's the amount of ownership that has been accumulated by the owner through mortgage payments and appreciation.

If you decide to obtain a 30 year loan, your monthly payments will be lower. However, just remember that lower monthly payments mean it will take longer to pay off the mortgage. Also, your equity will increase quite slowly. Why? During the early years of the 30 year loan most of the monthly payment will be used to pay the interest on the loan. Only a small portion of the monthly payment will be used to reduce the principal balance.

Another consideration is the total amount of interest that will be paid over the life of a 15 year loan vs. a 30 year loan. Do you think you will pay more interest on a 15 year loan or a 30 year loan? If you guessed that you will pay more interest over the life of a 30 year loan you're right! Let's look at an example: Assume that you can get a $200,000 15 year loan for 5% and a $200,000 30 year loan for 5.5%. Over the life of the 15 year loan you will pay $83,504.43 in interest. Over the life of the 30 year loan you will pay $206,942.90 in interest. The difference is significant! Some people obtain a 30 year loan and pay it off earlier than 30 years by making extra payments on the principal each month. This is certainly an approach you can take especially if you are disciplined enough to follow through.

> The decision between a 15-year mortgage and a 30-year mortgage isn't always simple. The 30-year mortgage has lower monthly payments, yet ultimately costs more; the 15-year mortgage mortgage requires higher monthly payments, but builds equity faster. It can be a tough call.

*Source: www.bankrate.com*

## #8

## Should You Make A Down Payment?

WHEN YOU PURCHASE your home, should you make a down payment? There are different views, but my answer is yes! Those who do not favor down payments believe you should not put any of your own money toward the purchase of your home. They believe you should borrow the entire cost. Why do I disagree with this approach? First, if you borrow the entire cost or more than 80% of the cost of the house you will be required to pay PMI (private mortgage insurance). This adds an additional cost to your monthly mortgage payments. (Generally, it's 0.5 to 1.0% of the loan amount.) That's money down the drain! However, if you make a down payment equal to at least 20% of the purchase price of the home, you will not have to pay PMI.

> *A down payment can be an important part of making a major purchase like a home or car. A down payment is a sum of money that is subtracted from the purchase price. You then usually get a loan to cover the remaining cost.*

Second, making a down payment gives you immediate equity in the home. What is equity? Equity is the difference between the value of the home and the amount of debt you owe on a home. If you purchase a home that has a value of $200,000 and you make a $20,000

down payment, you will have immediate equity of $20,000 ($200,000 value minus $180,000 loan equals $20,000 equity.) The equity represents your ownership interest. Over the life of the loan, assuming that the value of your home either remains the same or increases, your equity will increase as well. If the value of your home decreases, your equity will decrease as well.

Third, if you make a down payment you will reduce the amount of money you will need to borrow to finance the purchase of the home. This means you are taking action to limit the amount of your total debt.

Fourth, by making a down payment, you will naturally lower your monthly mortgage payment. This means that a lower amount of your monthly income will be needed to cover house related costs and you will have money remaining to do other things such as saving and having some fun.

Last of all, many lenders will require you to make a down payment as a condition of providing you with a home loan. Your compliance will be mandatory. For this reason alone, it is best to be financially prepared to make a down payment.

> Be sure you can manage whatever kind of loan you obtain. Work out the numbers and determine if waiting and saving more for a down payment can help you meet other financial goals, or if using what you have on hand for a down payment is right for you.

*Source: www.lendingtree.com*

# #9
# Should You Obtain A Home Inspection And Home Warranty?

IF YOU HAVE NEVER purchased a home before, you may not be aware of the value of a home inspection. After you have made an offer on a house and before you close the deal, you should obtain a home inspection. Why? A home inspection may reveal any defects in the house or identify items needing repair. Once you are made aware of specific problems, you may ask the current owner to make necessary repairs. If the owner is unwilling to make repairs, you may want to consider lowering the price you are willing to pay for the home.

*A home inspection is perhaps the most important chapter in the home-buying process and can benefit both the buyer in understanding the condition of the house and the seller who wants to provide accurate disclosure information.*

What types of problems may be detected during a home inspection? Problems with the water heater, electrical issues, leaky roof, broken appliances, bad water pipes, and problems with heating and air conditioning systems to name a few. Do yourself a favor and spend the money necessary to obtain a thorough home inspection by a reputable inspector. Also, obtain a written report of the inspector's findings. You'll be glad you did.

In some parts of the country, you will also need to obtain a termite inspection. Termites are insects that eat wood. It would be a shame for you to get stuck with a home infested with termites.

Another item you may want to consider when you are negotiating the purchase of a home is a home warranty. You may ask the seller to pay the cost of the warranty. Home warranties generally last for a year after purchase and they allow you to obtain free repair of certain items in the home in the event they stop functioning. If the seller is unwilling to pay the premium for the home warranty, you may want to do so yourself. You may also have the option of renewing the warranty at the end of one year as long as you are willing to cover the cost of the premium.

## >>General Home Inspection Checklist Items<<

- *Structural Elements*. Construction of walls, ceilings, floors, roof and foundation.
- *Exterior Evaluation*. Wall covering, landscaping, grading, elevation, drainage, driveways, fences, sidewalks, fascia, trim, doors, windows, lights and exterior receptacles.
- *Roof and Attic*. Framing, ventilation, type of roof construction, flashing and gutters. It does not include a guarantee of roof condition nor a roof certification.
- *Plumbing*. Identification of pipe materials used for potable, drain, waste and vent pipes, including condition. Toilets, showers, sinks, faucets and traps. It does not include a sewer inspection.
- *Systems and Components*. Water heaters, furnaces, air conditioning, duct work, chimney, fireplace and sprinklers.
- *Electrical*. Main panel, circuit breakers, types of wiring, grounding, exhaust fans, receptacles, ceiling fans and light fixtures.
- *Appliances*. Dishwasher, range and oven, built-in microwaves, garbage disposal and, yes, even smoke detectors.

*Source: answers.yahoo.com*

# #10
## What Is The Importance Of An Appraisal?

WHEN YOU PURCHASE a house and seek a loan to cover the purchase price, the house will need to be appraised. What is an appraisal? An appraisal is an official determination of the value of the home you are purchasing. Which factors are considered in an appraisal? The condition of the home, both inside and outside, the price for which other homes in the neighborhood recently sold, and the size of the home, to name a few.

*Appraisals are an important part of your home buying transaction. A real estate appraisal helps to establish a property's market value–the likely sales price it would bring if offered in an open and competitive real estate market.*

The appraisal will be required by your lender and you will be expected to cover the fee for the appraisal. If you are not asked to pay the appraisal fee up front, it will be included in your closing costs. Why is an appraisal needed? An appraisal is needed so that the lender can determine the maximum amount of money that should be loaned to you for the purchase of the home. The lender may or may not be willing to loan you the entire value of the home. Also, the lender likely will not loan you more than the appraised value of the home. Could this be a problem? Maybe, here's why. If you want to purchase a house that's selling for $275,000 and

the appraised value of the house is $250,000, the absolute highest loan you will likely be able to obtain is $250,000. If you still want to purchase the home, you will either have to try to negotiate with the seller to lower the price of the home by $25,000 or make a least a $25,000 down payment.

You may be wondering why the lender will not loan you any more than the appraisal value of the home. Remember, this is an investment for the lender. The loan to you is secured by the mortgage the lender will hold on the property. The lender wants to be in a position to get its money (investment) back if you fail to make your payments on the home loan. There is not much benefit to the lender in giving you a loan that is worth more than the value of the home you are buying. Here's a tip: make sure the price you negotiate to pay for a house is not greater than its appraised value. Even though you may love the house, you don't want to pay more for a home than it is worth.

>>*About Appraisers and Appraisals*<<

- Appraisers are licensed by individual states after completing coursework and internship hours that familiarize them with their real estate markets.
- The lender might use an appraiser on its staff, or contract with an independent appraiser. If you are allowed to choose the appraiser, and it isn't someone the lender is familiar with, the results might be subject to review before they are accepted.
- The appraiser should be an objective third party, someone who has no financial or other connection to any person involved in the transaction.
- The property being appraised is called the *subject property*.
- You will probably pay for the appraisal when you apply for your loan.

*Source: homebuying.about.com*

## #11
## Should Property Taxes Be Paid Separately?

GENERALLY WHEN YOU PURCHASE a home, there are four items included in the monthly mortgage payment: principal, interest, property taxes and insurance on the home. The lender typically takes the portion of your monthly mortgage payment that is used to cover the homeowner's insurance and property taxes and puts it in a separate account, generally referred to as an escrow account. When the taxes and insurance are due to be paid, the lender makes these payments for you. You might think this is a nice thing for your lender to do. Actually, the lender is making a profit on your money while it is sitting in the separate account.

You may be wondering whether there is some way you can pay your property taxes and home insurance yourself, without using the lender as a middle man. The answer is maybe. If you make a request at the time you obtain your home loan, some lenders will allow you to be solely responsible for paying your homeowner's insurance and property taxes. Why is this

*County treasurer offices and your state's Department of Treasury can generally assist you in learning what options are allowed in your area. Visit their websites online or find their phone number in the phone book to speak with someone and get your questions answered. The following are possible ways for you to pay your property tax.*

beneficial to you? First, it will reduce your monthly payment because now your monthly payment will only consist of the principal and interest on the loan. Second, it will allow you, not your lender, to accumulate interest on the money you set aside to pay the property taxes and homeowner's insurance premium. However, this arrangement is not for everyone! Only those who are disciplined enough to set aside the necessary funds to pay the property taxes and insurance should consider this option. If you lack this discipline, it would be better for you to make one payment to the lender and have the lender assume the responsibility of ensuring all appropriate payments are made.

There are several ways to pay your property tax. Here are a few:

1. **Pay property tax online**. An increasing number of Americans are paying taxes online, and property tax is no exception. Visit the website of your state government office overseeing taxation; there, you can determine whether online payment is an option.
2. **Pay property tax by phone**. The same credit or debit card can be used to pay property tax by phone, if your local municipality allows it. As with online payment, have your property tax statement handy so that you can provide all of the necessary information precisely.
3. **Pay by mail**. Payment of this nature must be made in the form of a check made payable to a local government office as per the instructions on the statement.
4. **Pay monthly**. Many seize the opportunity to pay a portion of their annual property tax each month as part of a monthly mortgage payment . If you choose to pay property tax in this fashion and your mortgage company has requested to receive your statements, you will not receive a property tax statement in the mail.

*Source: www.howtodothings.com*

## #12

## Should You Set Aside Money For Decorating, Furnishing And Home Improvements?

AS YOU ARE CONSIDERING the purchase of your home, remember that once you move in you will want to decorate. Why is it important to keep this in mind? You may think the only cost associated with owning a home is the monthly mortgage payment. Not so! You will want to create a comfortable and attractive home. This may require you to do such things as installing shutters, blinds or other window treatments, painting or wall papering, sanding and polishing hard wood floors, and doing many other things to make your home enjoyable.

What about furniture? If you're moving into your first home or buying a bigger home, you may want to buy additional furniture. Furniture costs can add up quickly. And what about that nice big flat screen T.V. you've had your eyes on? Cha-ching, cha-ching.

Home improvement costs are another category of costs you need to keep in mind. You may decide you don't like the kitchen counter top or some of the kitchen appliances. Perhaps

> *Everyone who owns a home, no matter if it is new or 100 years old, needs to create a special savings account to cover the cost of future home repairs. Accountants often call this a sinking fund because you need to make regular payments into a fund whose proceeds will pay off a future expense or expenses. The trouble is, many people do not set aside enough money each month and they do not raise the monthly payment each year to account for inflation.*

you want to update a bathroom or improve the landscaping in the front yard. These necessary or desirable improvement costs should be taken into consideration.

As you can see, all of these decorating, furniture and improvement costs can add up quickly. Just be mindful of this as you purchase your home. Be sure you have some cash reserves set aside to handle these expenses. Also, take your time and be patient. You don't have to have everything just the way you want it the first year you are in the house.

>>*Sample Budget Spreadsheet for Future Expenses*<<

|  | Remaining Life in Years | Current Replacement Cost | Average Inflation Rate | Future Cost | Monthly Set Aside |
|---|---|---|---|---|---|
| Roof | 10 | $2,175 | 1.5% | $2,524 | $21.03 |
| HVAC | 13 | $4,500 | 1.5% | $5,461 | $35.01 |
| Refrigerator | 6 | $750 | 1.5% | $820 | $11.39 |
| Oven | 6 | $900 | 1.5% | $984 | $13.67 |
| Washer | 8 | $525 | 1.5% | $591 | $6.16 |
| Dryer | 8 | $475 | 1.5% | $535 | $5.57 |
| Exterior Painting | 6 | $3,750 | 1.5% | $4,100 | $56.95 |
| Windows | 15 | $12,000 | 1.5% | $15,003 | $83.35 |
| Doors | 15 | $5,500 | 1.5% | $6,876 | $38.20 |
| Driveway | 9 | $4,200 | 1.5% | $4,802 | $44.47 |
| Water Heater | 8 | $900 | 1.5% | $1,014 | $10.56 |

Source: www.askthebuilder.com

# #13

## What Are Appreciation And Depreciation?

BE SURE YOU HAVE an understanding of the words appreciation and depreciation as they relate to owning a house. Appreciation occurs when the value of a house increases over time. A house may appreciate for several reasons. First, the neighborhood where the house is located may have become more desirable as a place to live. This may be due to new businesses in the area, better schools, or the overall stability of the neighborhood. Second, a house may also improve in value because of improvements made such as updating the kitchen or a bathroom or perhaps revamping the landscaping to provide greater curb appeal.

*Call a local real estate office and ask for a Comparative Market Analysis of the neighborhood. This will tell you the current value of the property. Also check with city planning to see if there are any new developments or plans in place which may attract people to the area.*

Houses, of course, do not always appreciate in value; sometimes they depreciate. What is depreciation? Depreciation occurs when the value of a house declines over time. Depending on the extent of the depreciation, the value may decline so low that it's worth less than what you paid for it. What are some of the causes of depreciation? If the house is not maintained by painting or repairing any defects,

it may depreciate. Also, if updates are not made to make the house attractive to prospective buyers, this could result in depreciation. An increase in neighborhood crime or other undesirable activities in the surrounding community may affect house value as well. Sometimes if there are a lot of houses for sale in a particular neighborhood, this too could impact house value.

Last but not least, remember that one of the most important factors in determining house value is **location, location, location**. Look for a house in a neighborhood that is friendly, safe, and clean. Also, having good schools nearby is always a plus. If you focus on location, you will be well on your way to purchasing a home that should increase in value over the years.

## >>*Percentage of Appreciation and Depreciation are NOT Equal*<<

It's a good thing when your home appreciates by 10%. When a $250,000 home appreciates by 10% it's value increases to $275,000.

But what happens when a home depreciates by 10%. Are you back where you started? No. A percentage price increase is always less than the same percentage price decrease.

Take the $250,000 home that appreciates to $275,000 because of a 10% appreciation rate. If the home depreciates from $275,000 by 10% it's value has fallen by $27,500 to $247,500.

In fact, a price drop of 9% erases a previous appreciation of 10%. And a price drop of just 16.66% eliminates a previous appreciation of 20%.

*Source: www.wheatworks.com*

# #14
# What Are Closing Costs?

WHEN YOU PURCHASE a house you will be required to pay closing costs. What are these costs? Closing costs are additional fees and expenses you will be required to pay when you finalize the purchase of your home. These costs will be approximately 3% to 7% of the value of the loan you will obtain to purchase the house. For example, if you obtain a $200,000 loan to purchase a house that costs $225,000, your closing costs may range between $6,000 and $14,000.

Closing costs vary and include such items as application fee, loan origination fee, points, appraisal fee, prepaid interest, homeowner's insurance, title search, lender's title insurance, recording fees, pest inspection, and settlement fees, to name a few. You will find your closing costs listed in detail on the HUD-1 settlement statement. This statement will be presented to you during the closing process.

Prior to the purchase of your home you may want to have some cash available to be used for the purpose of paying closing costs. Another approach you may want to use is to increase the

*Ways to Cut Closing Costs*

1. Shop around for lenders
2. Reduce fees not performed by 3rd parties
3. Go for a zero-point option or reducing points
4. Close later in the month
5. Negotiate with the home sellers
6. Shop around for mortgage brokers
7. Talk to your Realtor
8. Beware of "junk" or "garbage" fees

amount of your home loan so that it includes enough to cover the closing costs. However, this option is not always available. Besides, when you include the closing costs in the amount of the loan you are seeking, you will be increasing the amount of money you are borrowing to finance the purchase of the house.

Is there some other way to pay for closing costs? Yes. You may request the seller of the home you are purchasing to pay some or all of the closing costs. You will have to negotiate this with the seller. Depending on how motivated the seller is, he or she may be open to the idea of paying a portion of the closing costs. Is there some particular advantage to getting the seller to pay your closing costs? Yes. This will require you to have less cash on hand when you finalize the purchase of your home.

Here's the next question: would it be better for you to pay a higher price for the house and have the seller pay a portion of the closing costs OR pay a lower price for the house and cover the closing costs yourself?

>>*Let's look at an example*<<

Assume you and the seller have negotiated a price of $225,000 for a house. The closing costs you will be required to pay are expected to be $5,000 when you finalize the purchase. If instead you agreed to pay $230,000 for the house and have the seller pay the $5,000 of closing costs you will come out ahead financially. Why? You will not have to cough up $5,000 cash to close the deal. You can keep your $5,000 in your pocket or better yet, invest it for the long term. Yes, your monthly mortgage payments on the $230,000 loan will be a little higher than they would have been on a $225,000 loan. But the difference will be insignificant since you will be financing the payment of the additional $5,000 over a 15 year period or longer. Here's the point: when it comes to closing costs, it's usually a good idea to negotiate with the seller to get him to pay some or all of your closing costs.

## *Glossary*

**Adjustable Rate Mortgage**— a mortgage that provides for periodic changes in the interest rate, based on changing market conditions. *Abbreviation:* ARM

**Amortization** - The operation of paying off indebtedness, such as a mortgage, by installments. The conventional amortization periods are 15 or 30 years.

**Amortized mortgage**— A mortgage requiring periodic payments that include both interest and principal.

**Closing**—The conclusion of the sales transaction when the seller transfers title to the buyer in exchange for consideration.

**Closing costs**—Costs the buyer must pay at the time of the closing in addition to the down payment which may include points, title charges, credit report fee, document preparation fee, mortgage insurance premium, inspections, appraisals, prepayments for property taxes, deed recording fee, and homeowners insurance. Closing costs can vary considerably from one financial institution to another.

**Closing statement**—A detailed written summary of the financial settlement of a real estate transaction, showing all charges and credits made, and all cash received and paid out.

**Credit limit** -The maximum amount that you can borrow under a home equity plan.

**Credit report** - An account of your credit history, prepared by a credit bureau. A credit report will contain both credit history, such as what you owe to whom and whether you make the payments on time, as well as personal history, such as your former addresses, employment record and lawsuits in which you have been involved. An estimated 50% of all credit reports contain errors, such as accounts that don't belong to you, an incorrect account status or information reported that is older than seven years (ten years in the case of a bankruptcy).

**Credit score**—In the mortgage lending world, credit scores either make or break you when it comes to obtaining a home mortgage or getting the best rate you can. There are three different scores available to a mortgage lender each being generated by the three different credit agencies. The most popular, known as a Fico score is from Experian (formally TRW), then there is a Beacon score from Equifax, and finally a Emperica score from Trans Union. This is the "mortgage scoring" system used to get a conventional mortgage.

**Equity**—The difference in dollars between a house's value and the mortgage amount.

**Escrow**—A trust arrangement by which one or more parties deposit things of value with an authorized escrow agent in accordance with the terms of a real estate agreement.

**Origination fee** - A fee charged by lenders, in addition to interest, for services in connection with granting of a loan. Usually a percentage of the loan amount.

**PITI**—Principal, Interest, Taxes and Insurance.

**Private mortgage insurance (PMI)** - Default insurance on conventional loans, normally insuring the top 20%-25% of the loan and not the whole loan.

**Property taxes**—Taxes that are paid yearly on real property. Property taxes are ad valorem, based on the assessed value of the real property. Each taxing authority multiplies this appraised value by its annual tax rate.

**Real Estate Appraiser, licensed**—A person licensed to legally appraise real estate property for a fee.

**Underwriting**—The process of verifying data and approving a loan.

## Sources/Resources

1. www.hud.gov
2. www.mtsprofessor.com
3. www.daveramsey.com
4. www.wisegeek.com
5. www.loan.com
6. www.wikihow.com
7. www.bls.gov/k12/money05.htm
8. www.streetdirectory.com
9. www.money.cnn.com
10. www.federalreserve.gov
11. moneycentral.msn.com
12. www.bankrate.com
13. www.lendingtree.com
14. www.portland-homefinders.com
15. homebuying.about.com
16. www.howtodothings.com
17. www.askthebuilder.com
18. www.wheatworks.com
19. www.realestate.yahoo.com

## About the Author
## Pam Pitts

Pam Pitts is President of Butterfly Financial, LLC, a provider of financial education. As a licensee of The EDSA Group, Inc., Pam is certified to lead The EDSA Group, Inc workshops.

For five years, Pam served as an officer in the United States Navy. Later, she worked as an attorney in Nashville, Tennessee. Pam began her career with FedEx Corporation in 1992 as a Labor and Employment attorney. Subsequently she was promoted to the positions of Senior Employment Litigation Attorney, Managing Director of Labor and Employment Law, and Vice President Human Resources Services and Diversity. Nine of her fifteen years with the company involved working in challenging leadership roles where she was required to speak to many organizations within and outside the company. Pam left her successful career with FedEx Corporation in 2007 to pursue her passion regarding personal financial literacy.

To demonstrate her commitment to financial literacy, Pam completed courses necessary to become a financial planner and passed the national certified financial planner examination. Pam is using this knowledge to make a difference in the area of financial literacy. She is an impassioned advocate of financial literacy for all.

Pam graduated from Vanderbilt University with an engineering degree and she received her law degree from Catholic University in Washington, D.C.
She is a member of the Tennessee Bar, Society of Human Resource Management, the Memphis Chapter of the American Society of Training and Development , Toastmasters International, the Tennessee Chapter of the National Speakers Association as well as the Memphis Chapter of the Financial Planning Association.

Pam is also the author of *Money 101: 14 Things Every Teen Should Know About Money*. Money 101 provides money tips to assist teens in creating a rewarding financial life. The information provided encourages teens to develop great money habits and avoid making common money mistakes. Her second book, *The Awakening: Is This Your Financial Life?,* uses 20 pages of full-color illustrations to depict emotional aspects of a family's financial life. Intended to emphasize self-awareness and personal financial responsibility, the book is a tool for those who want to enhance their financial wellness and is designed to promote the life-long benefits of financial self-control.

www.ingramcontent.com/pod-product-compliance
Lightning Source LLC
Chambersburg PA
CBHW041808040426
42449CB00001B/6